The Number

by Emilio Delgado
illustrated by Jamie Smith

 HOUGHTON MIFFLIN   BOSTON

Printed in China

ISBN 10: 0-618-88676-1
ISBN 13: 978-0-618-88676-0

16 17 18 19 20 0940 21 20 19 18 17
4500648152

Andy: Welcome to "The Number Machine." Our last player spun 125. Can our next player spin a greater number? Hi Cindy. What's your favorite number?

Cindy: I have two favorite numbers. 6 and 7.

Andy: Let's spin the hundreds wheel.
Are you ready?

Cindy: I'm ready.

Andy: Round and round it goes.
Where will it stop?

Read • Think • Write How many hundreds, tens, and ones are on the big board now?

3

Andy: A 1! Fantastic!

Cindy: Oooo! Thanks, Bill.

Andy: Let's put a 1 on the Big Board.

Read • Think • Write What's the value of the 1 on the Big Board?

4

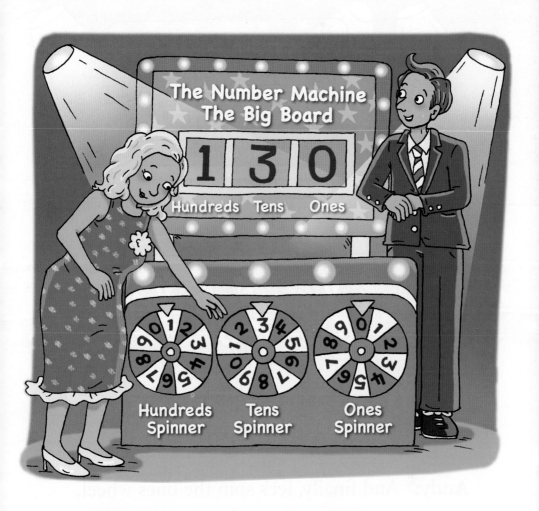

Andy: Now spin the tens wheel.

Cindy: 3! That's a good number!

Andy: We'll put a 3 up on the Big Board.

Read • Think • Write What is the value of the 3 on the Big Board?

Andy: And finally, let's spin the ones wheel.

Cindy: A 7! That's one of my favorite numbers.

Andy: Fantastic! 1, 3, and 7—or 137.

Cindy: What a great number!

Read • Think • Write What is the value of 7 on the Big Board?

6

Andy: It's a winning number.

Cindy: I spun a greater number!

Andy: Congratulations!

Read • Think • Write Which has the greater value, a 3 on the tens wheel or a 7 on the ones wheel?

Number Signs

Show

Look at page 3. Draw one of the spinners on the Number Machine to show the different digits Cindy might spin.

Share

Predict Talk about what will probably happen as Cindy spins each wheel on the Number Machine.

Write

Look at page 6. Write the three-digit number Cindy spun.